INTRODUCTION

The Passover story is the Jewish people's original story of becoming strangers in a strange land. It is the story that reminds us that we, too, have stood in the shoes of refugees and asylum seekers in search of safety and liberty.

With more displaced people around the world than at any time in recorded history, the words of the Haggadah are more poignant and relevant than ever before. As we read these words, we are commanded to put ourselves back into the narrative, to consider ourselves as though we, too, went out from Egypt, from the narrow place. We do this so that we may rise up renewed in our commitment to stand together as a thriving American Jewish movement supporting today's refugees and asylum seekers.

On Passover, we have the opportunity to remind ourselves *why* we do this work – to remind ourselves that this is our sacred obligation, amplified by our historic communal experience.

As we lift our voices in song and prayer, we call out together with those who long to be free. This year, there are still many who struggle towards liberation; next year, may we all be free.

Mark Hetfield
President and CEO

SHOES ON THE DOORSTEP

Before you begin the Seder, either walk with your guests to the front door or have one guest rise from the table and walk to the front door. There, place a pair of shoes on the doorstep and read the words below.

Leader: The heart of the Passover Seder tells the story of the Jewish people's exodus from slavery in Egypt. During the retelling of this story, we say the words, "אֲרַמִּי אֹבֵד אָבִי (*Arami oved avi*)." This phrase is sometimes translated as "My father was a wandering Aramean" and other times as "An Aramean sought to destroy my father." Somewhere between the two translations lies the essence of the Jewish experience: a rootless people who have fled persecution time and time again.

Group: When we recite the words "*Arami oved avi*," we acknowledge that we have stood in the shoes of the refugee. Today, as we celebrate our freedom, we commit ourselves to continuing to stand with contemporary refugees and asylum seekers. In honor of this commitment, we place a pair of shoes on the doorstep of our home to acknowledge that none of us is free until all of us are free and to pledge to stand in support of welcoming those who do not yet have a place to call home.

 **KADESH**

Pour the first cup of wine and recite the blessing below as a group:

וְהוֹצֵאתִי אֶתְכֶם ...   *V'hotzeiti etchem ...*   I will free you ...

As we remember our own liberation from bondage in Egypt, we express gratitude for the ability to work as God's partners in continued and continual redemption for today's refugees and asylum seekers. As our wine cups overflow in this moment of joy, we hold out hope for the day when every person in search of refuge in every corner of the earth can recall a story of freedom, reflect on a journey to security from violence and persecution, and no longer yearn for a safe place to call home. Blessed are You, Adonai our God, who frees those who are oppressed.

בָּרוּךְ אַתָּה יְיָ,   *Baruch Atah Adonai,*   Blessed are You, our God,
אֱלֹהֵינוּ מֶלֶךְ הָעוֹלָם,   *Eloheinu Melech ha'olam,*   Ruler of the Universe, who
בּוֹרֵא פְּרִי הַגָּפֶן.   *borei p'ree hagafen.*   creates the fruit of the vine.

Drink the first cup of wine.

URCHATZ

To begin the Seder, each guest may ritually wash their hands by pouring water over each hand three times, alternating between them. No blessing is recited. After everyone has washed, if all are comfortable, join hands and, together, read the passage below.

We begin our Seder by washing our hands, preparing ourselves to reach back into the original refugee story of the Jewish people. As we consider our own history of escaping violence and persecution at the hands of a merciless tyrant, we also reach forward to those still in need of protection: the more than 68 million displaced people around the world today. In particular, we extend our hands in welcome to those who continue to seek asylum in our country, and we remember the danger of what happens when ordinary people do not stand up to those in seats of power. Now, we join hands to recognize that the work of welcome is the work of each of us and all of us and that we are strongest together.

KARPAS

Leader: Centuries ago, only those who were free enjoyed the luxury of dipping their food to begin a meal. In celebration of our people's freedom, tonight, we, too, start our meal by dipping green vegetables. However, we also remember that our freedom came after tremendous struggle. And, so, we dip our vegetables into salt water to recall the ominous waters that threatened to drown our Israelite ancestors as they fled persecution in Egypt, as well as the tears they shed on that harrowing journey to freedom.

We recognize that, today, there are more than 68 million people still making these treacherous journeys away from persecution and violence in their homelands. As we dip the karpas into salt water tonight, we bring to mind those who have risked and sometimes lost their lives in pursuit of safety and liberty.

Group: We dip for the Rohingya father who walked for six days to avoid military capture in his native Myanmar before he came to the Naf River and swam to Bangladesh.[1]

We dip for the Syrian mother rescued from the dark waters of the Mediterranean Sea in the early hours of morning, still holding the lifeless body of her infant child after their small boat capsized.[2]

We dip for the Somali and Ethiopian refugees deliberately drowned when the smuggler who promised them freedom forced them into the Arabian Sea.[3]

Leader: We dip for these brave souls and for the thousands of other refugees and asylum seekers who have risked their lives in unsafe and unforgiving waters across the globe this past year.

It is a green vegetable that we dip tonight – a reminder of spring, hope, and the possibility of redemption even in the face of unimaginable difficulty. As we mourn those who have lost their lives in search of freedom, we remain hopeful that those who still wander will find refuge.

Group:

בָּרוּךְ אַתָּה יי,
אֱלֹהֵינוּ מֶלֶךְ הָעוֹלָם,
בּוֹרֵא פְּרִי הָאֲדָמָה.

Baruch Atah Adonai,
Eloheinu Melech ha'olam,
borei p'ri ha'adamah.

Blessed are You, our God, Ruler of the Universe, who creates the fruit of the earth.

Eat the parsley dipped in salt water.

YACHATZ

Take the middle matzah of the three on your Seder plate. Break it into two pieces. Wrap the larger piece, the afikomen, in a napkin and hide it sometime between now and the end of the meal. As you hold up the remaining smaller piece, read these words together:

We now hold up this broken matzah, which so clearly can never be repaired. We eat the smaller part while the larger half remains out of sight and out of reach for now. We begin by eating this bread of affliction and, then, only after we have relived the journey through slavery and the exodus from Egypt, do we eat the *afikomen*, the bread of our liberation. We see that liberation can come from imperfection and fragmentation. Every day, refugees and asylum seekers across the globe experience the consequences of having their lives ruptured, and, yet, they find ways to pick up the pieces and forge a new, if imperfect, path forward.

Choose one or more of the readings below to read aloud:

ART AND EDUCATION BLOOM IN THE DESERT

The world's refugee camps are some of the most desolate backdrops against which people fleeing violence and persecution rebuild their lives. The Akre Refugee Camp in Iraq, which houses more than a thousand Syrian families, was built out of the remains of a former Saddam Hussein prison. The Za'atari Refugee Camp in Jordan, one of the world's most populous refugee camps, consists of endless rows of beige tents and caravans with almost no plant or animal life. Dust storms, heat, and blindingly bright sunlight make life unbearable for the tens of thousands of primarily Syrian residents. Without much structured activity or access to education, the thousands of children in these camps sit listlessly. Initiatives like the Za'atari Project and the Castle Art Project change this bleak reality. Through these projects, children paint vividly colored murals on the walls of their temporary homes. They begin to work through the trauma they have experienced and to articulate and depict their dreams in technicolor. These projects create a sense of camaraderie and community amongst the participants and even provide a venue for the volunteers who run them to provide informal classes on water conservation, camp hygiene, and conflict resolution, in addition to artistic techniques.[4]

Overcoming Language Barriers

Many refugees find themselves in multiple countries before they find a permanent place to begin rebuilding their lives. If they do not speak the language in those countries, refugees face even greater challenges finding employment, and everyday tasks like filling out forms or trying to purchase food can feel nearly impossible. Children confront language barriers in school. The language of instruction may be the language of the child's host country – the country to which s/he flees – or it may be the language of their original homeland. This can differ from country to country. One refugee child followed by the Migration Policy Institute experienced a Tanzanian curriculum in English and Swahili during primary school, a Burundian curriculum officially in French and Kirundi but taught in English and Kiswahili during the beginning of secondary school, and a Congolese curriculum taught in French at the end of secondary school. This exposure to multiple languages ultimately can lead to the academic mastery of none.[5] Despite these obstacles, many refugees are beating the odds. In the Harran and Akcakale camps near the border of Syria, elderly women are teaching themselves how to read and thereby inspiring the younger women in the camp to learn new skills in order to sustain themselves.[6] Adam Sakhr, a Sudanese refugee who faced execution due to his political and religious views, used the difficulties he experienced when he first arrived in France to create an app called Nowall. Newly arrived refugees can send a text message through the app and then receive translation via their mobile phone in the form of a text message, phone call, or face to face meeting with a volunteer interpreter, depending on their need.[7]

Finding Work Amidst Discrimination

The 1951 Refugee Convention[8] clearly states that host countries must permit asylum seekers and refugees to engage in both wage-earning and self-employment. According to asylum experts, "the right has been recognized to be so essential to the realization of other rights that without the right to work, all other rights are meaningless."[9] Even with these legal protections, though, outside of the United States, "many of the world's refugees, both recognized and unrecognized, are effectively barred from accessing safe and lawful employment."[10] Despite these challenges, refugees are finding innovative ways to sustain themselves. Paola,[11] a refugee from Jurado, Colombia now living in Jaqué, Panama, started a small business selling tamales with a local Panamanian woman. However, she found that it was difficult to survive and support herself and her grandchildren on the income from tamale-making alone. When she heard about HIAS' livelihood initiatives to help local refugees learn new sustainable jobs, she submitted a proposal to build a chicken coop and received a grant to seed a successful small chicken farm. She says that this new work has helped her regain some of her dignity and gives her a sense of control that was taken away when she had to flee her home.

MAGID

The Magid – the story of the Israelites' journey from slavery to freedom – now begins. Group:

עֲבָדִים הָיִינוּ
לְפַרְעֹה בְּמִצְרָיִם

*Avadim hayinu
l'Pharaoh b'Mitzrayim.*

We were slaves
to Pharaoh in Egypt.

As we retell our story, we hold in our minds and inscribe on our hearts the stories of the millions of people across the globe who still yearn to be free.

Pour the second cup of wine.

HA LACHMA ANYA

Leader:

הָא לַחְמָא עַנְיָא דִּי
אֲכָלוּ אַבְהָתָנָא בְּאַרְעָא
דְמִצְרָיִם. כָּל דִּכְפִין
יֵיתֵי וְיֵיכֹל, כָּל דִּצְרִיךְ
יֵיתֵי וְיִפְסַח. הָשַׁתָּא
הָכָא, לְשָׁנָה הַבָּאָה
בְּאַרְעָא דְיִשְׂרָאֵל. הָשַׁתָּא
עַבְדֵי, לְשָׁנָה הַבָּאָה
בְּנֵי חוֹרִין.

Ha lachma anyah di achalu av'hatanah v'ar'ah d'Mitzrayim. Kol dich'fin yay-tay v'yaichol, kol ditzrich yay-tay v'yifsach. Hashatah hacha, l'shanah ha'ba'ah b'ar'ah d'Yisrael. Hashatah avdei, l'shanah ha'ba'ah b'nei chorin.

This is the bread of affliction, the poor bread, that our ancestors ate in the land of Egypt. Let all who are hungry come and eat, all who are in need come and celebrate Passover with us. This year we are here; next year we will be in Israel. This year we are slaves; next year we will be free.

Participant: In fall 2015, with the Syrian refugee crisis making headlines on a daily basis, Melina Macall and Kate McCaffrey each reached out to their rabbi, Elliott Tepperman, to find out how the Jewish community in their New Jersey town was responding. He connected the two, and they teamed up to start the Syria Supper Club in an attempt to change the narrative around refugees. Their first program brought Syrian refugees and members of the local Jewish community together for the "traditional" Jewish version of Christmas dinner: Chinese food.

The two organizers then saw a chance to create a platform for breaking down stereotypes and building mutual understanding in the midst of an often toxic debate around refugees. With food and camaraderie as the common denominators, Macall and McCaffrey conceived of the supper club as a way to create additional pathways to increased independence for resettled refugees in their community who were just getting on their feet in a new country. They also wanted to encourage more people to seek out first-hand encounters with refugees beyond what they read in the news.

The duo began hosting dinners at which refugee cooks would prepare the meal for an assortment of guests. Proceeds go toward supporting the cooks and their families as they begin their new lives. More than 100 dinners later, they have dozens of cooks eager to participate, and the dinners often sell out several weeks in advance.

"On the one hand, you can look at this and just say, 'Hey, it's just a dinner party,'" explains Macall. "And on the other hand, you can say, 'You know what? It's actually a radical act saying we have faith in humanity.'" [12]

Group: Meeting face to face and breaking bread together blurs the distance between a perceived "us" and "them," between "refugees" and "non-refugees." May all find themselves welcome at this table, regardless of how long they have called this country home.

FIRST QUESTION

Just like the Four Questions of the Passover Haggadah, which traditionally begin the Magid section of the Seder, this is the first of four alternative questions for discussion that you will find scattered throughout this Haggadah. These questions are meant to spark conversations that can happen throughout the Seder.

Participant: "When I found out I got into the University, I immediately called my 'real' mom in Afghanistan, whom I hadn't seen since I was 14. My family, which belongs to the Hazaras, lived under the constant threat of the Taliban, until, one day the latter tried to run me over with a car. My parents feared for my life, and sent me to Iran. At first I was crying all the time. It hurt too much being on my own. When things got tougher there too, I headed to Europe.

I was just 17 when I came once more close to dying, this time in my attempt to cross to Samos on a boat from Turkey, along with four more Afghans. I had never seen the sea before and although I knew how to swim, the waves terrified me. When the sea got really rough and the oars of the boat broke one after another, there was panic. I was rowing with all the strength I had in me. What kept me going was a 13-year-old boy who was constantly asking me *'If I fall in the sea, will you save me?' 'As long as I am alive, you have nothing to fear,'* I kept telling him. We are still good friends with this boy.

I love Thessaloniki, the town where I live now, but if I could, I would return to Afghanistan without second thoughts. My country is beautiful, there are amazing landscapes, natural resources and high mountains. The only thing missing is peace…"

— *Hamid, from Afghanistan, living in Greece in 2016*[13]

Discuss as a group:

Through the Passover Seder, we reconnect with our biblical journey to liberation, and, yet, we retell the story now mindful of those who are not yet free – those whose futures are, therefore, bound up in our future. We recognize, as Hamid does in this powerful narrative, that the way we live has bearing on the lives of those who are not yet free. Why do you think we retell this story each year? With an eye to the struggles of our time, whose future do you feel is bound up in yours?

FOUR CHILDREN

Below is a contemporary adaptation of the traditional Four Children from the Passover Haggadah. Read these words together and then discuss the question that follows:

The one who ignores...

She turns off the news and closes the newspaper, speechless as she considers the magnitude of the problem. "68 million displaced people?" she wonders, "It couldn't possibly be that many."

The one who deflects...

They want to attend the rally for refugees and sign that petition, but they lost track of time with so many other pressing issues demanding their attention. "Someone else will take this one," they console themselves, "I've got other priorities."

The one who abandons...

He knows that Jewish values command him to welcome the stranger, but he cannot reconcile that with his worries about the economy and his fear of terrorism. "It's not the same as when my grandparents came to this country," he says.

The ones who understand...

They see that the Jewish refugee story never really ends; our role in the story shifts. Together, they take actions big and small. While they know they cannot complete the work, they do not desist from trying to make a difference. "We used to help refugees because *they* were Jewish," they say, "But now we help refugees because *we* are Jewish."

Discuss as a group:

When we talk about the global refugee crisis, many of us may struggle to reconcile one or more of these voices within ourselves or we hear them in family members and friends. How do you respond to your own struggle when you think about taking action in support of refugees and asylum seekers? How do you respond to the concerns of others?

VEHI SHE'AMDA

Lift up second cup of wine.

Leader:

וְהִיא שֶׁעָמְדָה לַאֲבוֹתֵינוּ וְלָנוּ. שֶׁלֹּא אֶחָד בִּלְבָד עָמַד עָלֵינוּ לְכַלּוֹתֵנוּ, אֶלָּא שֶׁבְּכָל דּוֹר וָדוֹר עוֹמְדִים עָלֵינוּ לְכַלּוֹתֵנוּ, וְהַקָּדוֹשׁ בָּרוּךְ הוּא מַצִּילֵנוּ מִיָּדָם.

Vehi she'amda la'avoteinu v'lanu. She'lo echad bilvad amad aleinu l'chaloteinu, elah she'bechol dor vador omdim aleinu l'chaloteinu, V'Ha'Kadosh Baruch Hu matzileinu mi'yadam.

This is the promise that has sustained our ancestors and us. For not one enemy alone rose up to destroy us; rather, in every generation, they rise up to destroy us, and the Holy Blessed One rescues us from their hands.

Group: As a refugee people – an immigrant people – we know that anti-Jewish and anti-immigrant hatred are deeply entwined. Tonight, we retell the story of the moment when first these hatreds met thousands of years ago, as Pharaoh declared that the Israelites had become too numerous in Egypt. Sadly, this narrative has repeated itself throughout Jewish history and continues to be weaponized, often with lethal consequences.

Today, though, is the first moment in history when Jews are not predominately refugees. Rooted in our communal experience, in this generation, as in all generations before us, the Jewish people knows that our futures are bound up with those who now seek to enter our country, particularly refugees and asylum seekers fleeing violence and persecution. May no more generations suffer at the hands of those who vilify the other, and may we continue to be God's partners in the ongoing redemption of those who long for freedom.

Place second cup of wine down on the table without drinking.

10 PLAGUES

Remembering the ten plagues that God brought upon the Egyptians when Pharaoh refused to free the Israelites, we have the opportunity now to recognize that the world is not yet free of adversity and struggle. This is especially true for refugees and asylum seekers. After you pour out a drop of wine for each of the ten plagues that Egypt suffered, we invite you to then pour out drops of wine for ten modern plagues facing refugee communities worldwide and in the United States. After you have finished reciting the plagues, choose a few of the expanded descriptions to read aloud.

1
VIOLENCE

2
DANGEROUS JOURNEYS

3
POVERTY

4
FOOD INSECURITY

5
LACK OF ACCESS TO EDUCATION

6
XENOPHOBIA

7
ANTI-REFUGEE LEGISLATION

8
LANGUAGE BARRIERS

9
WORKFORCE DISCRIMINATION

10
LOSS OF FAMILY

VIOLENCE

Most refugees initially flee home because of violence that may include sexual and gender-based violence, abduction, or torture. The violence grows as the conflicts escalate. Unfortunately, many refugees become victims of violence once again in their countries of first asylum. A 2013 study found that close to 80% of refugees from the Democratic Republic of Congo (DRC) living in Kampala, Uganda had experienced sexual and gender-based violence either in the DRC or in Uganda.[14]

DANGEROUS JOURNEYS

Forced to flee their home due to violence and persecution, refugees may make the dangerous journey to safety on foot, by boat, in the back of crowded vans, or riding on the top of train cars. Over the last several years, the United States has seen record numbers of unaccompanied minors fleeing violence in Central America. Many of these children have survived unimaginably arduous journeys, surviving abduction, abuse, and rape. Erminia was just 15 years old when she came to the United States from El Salvador in 2013. After her shoes fell apart while she walked through the Texas desert, she spent three days and two nights walking in only her socks. "There were so many thorns," she recalls, "and I had to walk without shoes. The entire desert."[15]

LACK OF ACCESS TO EDUCATION

The 1951 Convention Relating to the Status of Refugees affirms that the right to education applies to refugees. However, research shows that refugee children face far greater language barriers and experience more discrimination in school settings than the rest of the population.[16] Muna, age 17 in 2016, a Syrian refugee living in Jordan, who dropped out of school, said, "We can't get educated at the cost of our self-respect."[17]

XENOPHOBIA

Just as a 1939 poll from the American Institute of Public Opinion found that more than 60% of Americans opposed bringing Jewish refugees to the United States in the wake of World War II, today we still see heightened xenophobia against refugees. This fear can manifest through workplace discrimination, bias attacks against Muslim refugees, anti-refugee legislation such as the American SAFE Act of 2015 (H.R. 4038) which passed the House but was thankfully defeated in the Senate, and the various Executive Orders issued in 2017 and 2018 to limit refugees' ability to come to the United States.

DAYEINU

Take turns reading aloud:

Dayeinu. It would have been enough. But would it have been enough?

If God had only parted the sea but not allowed us to cross to safety, would it have been enough? If we had crossed to freedom and been sustained wandering through the wilderness but not received the wisdom of Torah to help guide us, would it have been enough?

What is enough?

As we sing the traditional "Dayeinu" at the Passover Seder, we express appreciation even for incomplete blessings. We are reminded that, in the face of uncertainty, we can cultivate gratitude for life's small miracles, and we can find abundance amidst brokenness. Just as the story of our own people's wandering teaches us these lessons time and time again, so, too, do the stories of today's refugees and asylum seekers. The meager possessions they bring with them as they flee reflect the reality of rebuilding a life from so very little.

For Um, the blessing of being alive in Jordan after escaping violence in Homs in the company of her husband with only the clothes on her back – *Dayeinu*: it would have been enough.[18]

For Dowla, the wooden pole balanced on her shoulders, which she used to carry each of her six children when they were too tired to walk during the 10-day trip from Gabanit to South Sudan – *Dayeinu*: it would have been enough.

For Sajida, the necklace her best friend gave her to remember her childhood in Syria – *Dayeinu*: it would have been enough.

For Muhammed, scrolling through the list of numbers on his cell phone, his only connection to the people he has known his whole life – *Dayeinu*: it would have been enough.

For Magboola, the cooking pot that was small enough to carry but big enough to cook sorghum to feed herself and her three daughters on their journey to freedom – *Dayeinu*: it would have been enough.[19]

For Farhad, the photograph of his mother that he managed to hide under his clothes when smugglers told him to throw everything away as he escaped Afghanistan – *Dayeinu*: it would have been enough.[20]

Even as we give thanks for these small miracles and incomplete blessings in the world as it is, we know that this is not enough. We dream of the world as it could be. We long for a world in which safe passage and meager possessions blossom into lives rebuilt with enough food on the table, adequate housing, and sustainable jobs. We fight for the right of all people fleeing violence and persecution to be warmly welcomed into the lands in which they seek safety, their strength honored and their vulnerability protected. When these dreams become a reality, *Dayeinu*: it will have been enough.

SECOND QUESTION

Leader:

בְּכָל דּוֹר וָדוֹר	B'chol dor vador	In every generation,
חַיָּב אָדָם לִרְאוֹת	chayav adam lirot	everyone is obligated to see
אֶת עַצְמוֹ, כְּאִלּוּ	et atzmo, k'ilu	themselves as though
הוּא יָצָא מִמִּצְרָיִם.	hu yatza mi'Mitzrayim.	they personally left Egypt.

Discuss as a group:

Put yourself back into the story of the Exodus. What do you remember from leaving Egypt?

SECOND CUP OF WINE

Lift the second cup of wine and read together.

וְהִצַּלְתִּי אֶתְכֶם ...	V'hitzalti etchem ...	I will deliver you ...
בָּרוּךְ אַתָּה יי,	Baruch Atah Adonai,	Blessed are You, our God,
אֱלֹהֵינוּ מֶלֶךְ הָעוֹלָם,	Eloheinu Melech ha'olam,	Ruler of the Universe, who
בּוֹרֵא פְּרִי הַגָּפֶן.	borei p'ree ḥagafen.	creates the fruit of the vine.

Just as we remember all of the times throughout history when the nations of the world shut their doors on Jews fleeing violence and persecution in their homelands, so, too, do we remember with gratitude the bravery of those who took us in during our times of need – the Ottoman Sultan who welcomed Spanish Jews escaping the Inquisition, Algerian Muslims who protected Jews during pogroms initiated by the French Pied-Noir, and the righteous gentiles hiding Jews in their homes during World War II. Today, we aspire to stand on the right side of history as we ask our own government to take a leadership role in protecting the world's most vulnerable refugees and asylum seekers. May we find the bravery to open up our nation and our hearts to those who are in need. Blessed are You, Adonai our God, who delivers those in search of safety.

Drink the second cup of wine.

RACHTZAH

Each guest may ritually wash their hands by pouring water over each hand three times, alternating between them. Then, recite the blessing below together.

בָּרוּךְ אַתָּה יְיָ, אֱלֹהֵינוּ מֶלֶךְ הָעוֹלָם, אֲשֶׁר קִדְּשָׁנוּ בְּמִצְוֹתָיו וְצִוָּנוּ עַל נְטִילַת יָדָיִם.

Baruch Atah Adonai, Eloheinu Melech ha'olam, asher kid'shanu b'mitzvotav v'tzivanu al nitilat yadayim.

Blessed are You, Our God, Ruler of the Universe, who has sanctified us with commandments and has commanded us on the washing of hands.

Participant: As we pour water over our hands in anticipation for the meal to come, we are mindful of the many roles that water can play in our lives. At this moment, we use it to cleanse and prepare. But, for many around the world, water is the difference between life and death, between freedom and continued oppression. For the millions of asylum seekers worldwide who undertake treacherous journeys out of persecution, the oceans and seas are precarious pathways to liberty, often taking their lives in their depths. For the millions of refugees living in camps across the globe, access to clean water determines whether they will survive to rebuild their lives. We pray that all those in search of refuge find the transformative waters they need, encountering life renewed and anew.

MOTZI MATZAH

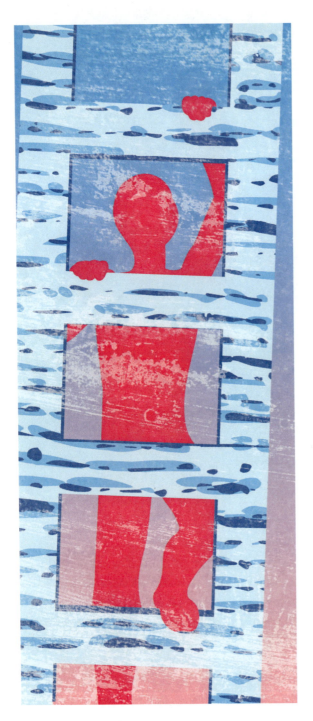

Leader:

At the Passover Seder, we eat matzah as we remember the modest means by which the Israelites sustained themselves on their journey out of slavery, enabling them to survive and thrive in their new homeland.

Like our ancestors, today's refugees rebuild their lives with precious few resources at their disposal. These meager resources often become the seeds of their liberation as they go on to lay down new roots, rebuild their lives, and make important contributions to their local communities and our country as a whole.

A participant reads the following story:

**Tashitaa Tufaa,
Ethiopian refugee living in Minnesota**

In 1992, at the age of 24, Tashitaa Tufaa came to the United States, where he sought political asylum. Though Tashitaa had earned a college degree in his native Ethiopia, when he came to the U.S., the only work he could find was as a dishwasher, making less than $6 per hour. In order to make ends meet, Tashitaa took on several jobs, including working as a taxi driver.

After almost a decade of working long, hard hours, Tashitaa challenged himself to start his own business. In 2003, he went door-to-door in his new home state of Minnesota to try to find clients for his new transportation business. Three years later, Tashitaa had successfully launched the Metropolitan Transportation Network (MTN). Started with just his taxi and his wife's minivan, this new company was so successful that Tashitaa was able to buy school buses; though, he had to pay for them in cash. Today, MTN is one of the largest bus companies in Minnesota, employing hundreds of people and generating tens of millions of dollars in income. In addition to running the business, Tashitaa also mentors refugees across the country to help them achieve financial self-sufficiency and success for themselves and their families.[21]

Take turns reading these facts aloud:

Did You Know?

- Though refugees living in the United States for five years or less have a median household income of roughly $22,000, that number more than triples in the following decades, growing far faster than other foreign-born groups.

- Refugees are taxpayers. Over a twenty-year period, the majority of refugees fully pay back the cost of resettlement and other related benefits. They contribute, on average, $21,324 more in taxes than any costs associated with their initial resettlement.

- Refugees across the United States are helping to revitalize Main Street. In Akron, Ohio, Bhutanese and Burmese refugees have transformed the North Hill neighborhood from a landscape of vacant storefronts into a bustling corridor of grocery stores, clothing vendors, and jewelry shops. Bosnian refugees in St. Louis have transformed a section of the city called Bevo Mill, once known for its high crime, into an area full of popular Bosnian-owned restaurants, bars, and cafes.[22]

Discuss one of the following questions together:

1 *Does Tashitaa's story resonate with your own family's story of coming to the United States?*

2 *How might you use Tashitaa's story or the facts above to respond to those who claim that refugees take more from the American economy than they contribute?*

When your discussion concludes, recite the following blessings as a group, distribute the top and middle matzot set aside earlier in the Seder, and then taste the matzah:

בָּרוּךְ אַתָּה יי, אֱלֹהֵינוּ מֶלֶךְ הָעוֹלָם, הַמּוֹצִיא לֶחֶם מִן הָאָרֶץ.	*Baruch Atah Adonai, Eloheinu Melech ha'olam, hamotzi lechem min ha'aretz.*	Blessed are You, our God, Ruler of the Universe, who brings forth bread from the earth.
בָּרוּךְ אַתָּה יי, אֱלֹהֵינוּ מֶלֶךְ הָעוֹלָם, אֲשֶׁר קִדְּשָׁנוּ בְּמִצְוֹתָיו וְצִוָּנוּ עַל אֲכִילַת מַצָּה.	*Baruch Atah Adonai, Eloheinu Melech ha'olam, asher kid'shanu b'mitzvotav v'tzivanu al achilat matzah.*	Blessed are You, our God, Ruler of the Universe, who sanctifies us with commandments and calls upon us to eat matzah.

MAROR

Group: With the taste of bitterness just before our lips, we remind ourselves of the bitterness that led to the enslavement of our ancestors in Egypt. Tonight, we force ourselves to experience the stinging pain of the *maror* so that we should remember that, appallingly, even centuries later, the bitterness of xenophobia still oppresses millions of people around the world, forcing them to flee their homes.

As we taste the bitter herbs, we vow not to let words of hatred pass through our own lips and to root out intolerant speech wherever we may hear it, so that no one should fall victim to baseless hatred.

| בָּרוּךְ אַתָּה יי, אֱלֹהֵינוּ מֶלֶךְ הָעוֹלָם, אֲשֶׁר קִדְּשָׁנוּ בְּמִצְוֹתָיו וְצִוָּנוּ עַל אֲכִילַת מָרוֹר. | *Baruch Atah Adonai, Eloheinu Melech ha'olam, asher kid'shanu b'mitzvotav v'tzivanu al achilat maror.* | Blessed are You, our God, Ruler of the Universe, who sanctifies us with commandments and calls upon us to eat bitter herbs. |

Eat the maror.

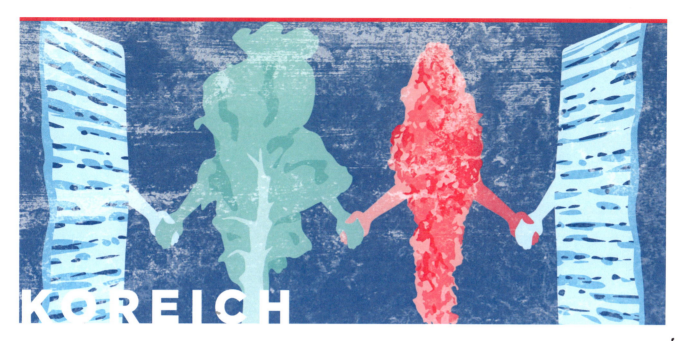

KOREICH

Group: We now prepare to build the Hillel sandwich, combining the bitter *maror* with the sweet *charoset*.

With the bitterness of the *maror* still stinging our tongues and the knowledge that fear of "the other" continues to displace people still stinging our hearts, we take comfort in knowing that there can be an antidote to that hatred. It is up to each of us to temper the hatred that still plagues our world by joining together and saying *"Dayeinu"* – it is, now, enough.

Combine maror and charoset between two pieces of matzah and recite the following as a group:

זֵכֶר לְמִקְדָּשׁ כְּהִלֵּל. כֵּן עָשָׂה הִלֵּל בִּזְמַן שֶׁבֵּית הַמִּקְדָּשׁ הָיָה קַיָּם. הָיָה כּוֹרֵךְ מַצָּה וּמָרוֹר וְאוֹכֵל בְּיַחַד, לְקַיֵּם מַה שֶּׁנֶּאֱמַר: עַל מַצּוֹת וּמְרוֹרִים יֹאכְלֻהוּ.	Zeicher l'mikdash k'Hillel. Kein asah Hillel biz'man shebeit hamikdash hayah kayam. Hayah koreich matzah umaror v'ochel b'yachad, l'kayeim mah shene-emar: Al matzot um'rorim yochluhu.	In memory of the Temple, according to Hillel. This is what Hillel would do when the Temple still existed: he would combine matzah and maror and eat them together, in order to fulfill the teaching, "with matzot and maror they shall eat [the Passover sacrifice]" (Numbers 9:11).

After you make the Hillel sandwich, discuss together:

Over the next year, what will you do to temper the bitterness of xenophobia, as well as anti-refugee and anti-Muslim hate?

Just before the meal is served, the group reads:

The egg that we place on the Seder plate is meant to remind us of the natural cycle of life – that, even after enormous suffering, we can experience renewal and rebirth. Just as the Jewish people not only survived but also thrived following our exodus from Egypt and the many persecutions and expulsions we experienced thereafter, so, too, do today's refugees rebuild their lives in extraordinary ways. Let us now read three of their stories.

Participants each read a story:

Evelyn Lauder (née Hausner), a native of Vienna, Austria, fled Nazi-occupied Europe with her family as a young child and came to the United States with HIAS' assistance. Shortly after starting her teaching career in Harlem, Evelyn met and married Leonard Lauder. After they were married, she joined the business founded by her mother-in-law: Estée Lauder Companies. She ultimately became Senior Corporate Vice President, created the Clinique brand, and developed its product line. Evelyn Lauder's philanthropy and passion brought breast cancer and women's health issues to the forefront of public awareness. She co-established The Breast Cancer Research Foundation, which formalized the pink ribbon as a worldwide symbol for breast cancer awareness and has raised over $350 million to support breast cancer research across the globe.

Having fled civil war in his native Liberia in 1994, **Wilmot Collins** came to this country as a refugee. In the days before he and his wife left Monrovia, food was so scarce they once ate toothpaste. Once resettled in the United States, Wilmot became a U.S. citizen and worked for the Montana Department of Health and Human Services, specializing in child protection. He has also been a member of the United States Navy Reserve. Today, he is mayor of Helena, Montana, having defeated a four-term incumbent mayor to become the first black person to be elected the mayor of any city in the history of Montana.[23]

Sam (Yamin) Yingichay grew up in Myanmar (formerly known as Burma) as one of an estimated 168 million children between the ages of 5 and 14 engaged in child labor around the world. Forced into constructing roads and living with an abusive stepfather, at 14, Yamin escaped and began to search for her birth father. Eventually, she met a man claiming to know her father and followed him to Thailand, where she was once again sold into hard labor. Holding onto hope that she would one day be free, Yamin survived and escaped to Malaysia where she was granted refugee status and accepted for resettlement to the United States. In 2008, Yamin arrived in Grand Haven, Michigan to live with a foster family. Today, Yamin is studying to become a nurse. She dreams of being able to support her family still living in Myanmar and to help other refugees in the United States.[24]

(*The Passover meal is served.*)

TZAFUN

As the meal is ending, the youngest participants – in body or spirit! – should go look for the afikomen, which was hidden earlier in the meal. Once it is found, read the passage below as the group shares in eating the afikomen.

Earlier in our Seder, we broke the middle matzah, hiding the larger piece out of sight. What was broken and out of reach to us now becomes our sustenance. As we share in the *afikomen*, we acknowledge that there are those who would ignore today's refugees and asylum seekers, overwhelmed by their suffering or even actively opposed to responding to their plight. Our sacred task, then, is to bring their stories into view and ensure that they are not hidden from the world's attention.

BARECH

If you wish to say the full birkat ha'mazon, you may select the text of your choosing from any bencher or prayer book.

Group:

בָּרוּךְ אַתָּה יְיָ, אֱלֹהֵינוּ מֶלֶךְ הָעוֹלָם, הַזָּן אֶת הָעוֹלָם כֻּלּוֹ בְּטוּבוֹ בְּחֵן בְּחֶסֶד וּבְרַחֲמִים, הוּא נוֹתֵן לֶחֶם לְכָל בָּשָׂר כִּי לְעוֹלָם חַסְדּוֹ.

Baruch Atah Adonai, Eloheinu Melech ha'olam, ha'zan et ha'olam kulo b'tuvo b'chen b'chesed u'v'rachamim, Hu notein lechem l'chol basar ki l'olam chasdo.

Blessed are You, Our God, Ruler of the Universe, who nourishes the entire universe with your goodness; in kindness, mercy, and compassion, You provide food to all living beings, for your love is everlasting.

Participant: We give thanks for the ability to retell our story through the symbolic foods we have eaten this evening. Indeed, we are not the only people for whom food is liberation. Together, we read the words of Nathaly Rosas Martinez, who grew up between Mexico and the United States, as we remember that the stories of the foods we eat remind us of who we are in this world, even when we have left home in search of safety and freedom.

Group:
I am from a place where
The food is an art and every bite
Is a spicy piece of our culture
Where the smells call you to enjoy
And the flavors take you to your memories.

Our food is not only food
It's a way to communicate our feelings
It's a way to talk with our family
It's our history, our identity.

Our kitchen table may be in another country
And the people who ate with us
Are no longer here,
But we will return to gather.[25]

Pour the third cup of wine.

THIRD CUP OF WINE ✓

Lift the third cup of wine and read together.

וְגָאַלְתִּי אֶתְכֶם ...   *V'ga'alti etchem ...*   I will redeem you ...

בָּרוּךְ אַתָּה יי, אֱלֹהֵינוּ מֶלֶךְ הָעוֹלָם, בּוֹרֵא פְּרִי הַגָּפֶן.   *Baruch Atah Adonai, Eloheinu Melech ha'olam, borei p'ree hagafen.*   Blessed are You, our God, Ruler of the Universe, who creates the fruit of the vine.

Emboldened to welcome refugees into our communities, may we remember that true welcome is not completed upon a person's safe arrival in our country but in all the ways we help people to rebuild their lives. As God provided for our needs on the long journey from slavery to the Promised Land, let us give the refugees in our communities the tools they need not just to survive but to thrive: safe homes to settle into, quality education for their children, English language tutoring, access to jobs, and all of the things we would want for ourselves and our families. Blessed are You, Adonai our God, who gives us the opportunity to be your partner in ongoing redemption.

Drink the third cup of wine.

THIRD QUESTION

Discuss as a group:

What do you think makes some people stay and continue to experience unimaginable trauma and others flee in search of refuge and asylum? Can you understand both ways of thinking?

23

KAVANAH FOR OPENING THE DOOR FOR ELIJAH

Have a participant open the door for Elijah. Make sure that all participants have an extra wine glass that has not been used for the previous three cups of wine and will not be used for the fourth cup of wine. Pour a cup of wine into the additional wine glass. Raising the additional cup of wine and read as a group:

Gathered around the Seder table, we ultimately pour four cups, remembering the gift of freedom that our ancestors received centuries ago. We delight in our liberation from Pharaoh's oppression.

We drink four cups for four promises fulfilled.

The first cup as God said, "I will free you from the labors of the Egyptians."

The second as God said, "And I will deliver you from their bondage."

The third as God said, "I will redeem you with an outstretched arm and with great judgments."

The fourth because God said, "I will take you to be My People."

We know, though, that all are not yet free. As we welcome Elijah the Prophet into our homes, we offer an additional cup, a cup not yet consumed.

An additional cup for the more than 68 million refugees and displaced people around the world still waiting to be free – from the refugee camps in Chad to the cities and towns of Ukraine, for the Syrian refugees still waiting to be delivered from the hands of tyrants, for the thousands of asylum seekers in the United States still waiting in detention for redemption to come, for all those who yearn to be taken in not as strangers but as fellow human beings.

This Passover, let us walk in the footsteps of the One who delivered us from bondage. When we rise from our Seder tables, may we be emboldened to take action on behalf of the world's refugees, hastening Elijah's arrival as we speak out on behalf of those who are not yet free.

Place this additional cup of wine down untasted.

Hallel is a time to offer words of praise and song. Consider singing some of your favorite songs about justice or read the words below. You may also consider singing "Pitchu Li" before you begin the reading.

Leader:

פִּתְחוּ לִי שַׁעֲרֵי צֶדֶק   *Pitchu li sha'arei tzedek*   Open for me the gates of
אָבֹא בָם אוֹדֶה יָהּ.   *avo vam odeh Yah.*   righteousness that I may
enter them and praise God.

Group: Open up the gates of freedom.
Open them to those in need of safety and protection.
Open up the gates of mercy.
Open them to those who forget that we were once strangers in the land of
   Egypt, the narrow place.
Open up the gates of justice.
Open them to those who remember that we know the soul of the stranger.
Open up the gates of righteousness.
Open them to those who walk hand-in-hand and heart-to-heart with today's
   refugees and asylum seekers.
Together, we will find the path to freedom.

Pour the fourth cup of wine.

FOURTH QUESTION

Discuss as a group:

Just as we open the door for Elijah, what or to whom do you want to open the door to in your own life this year? What fears do you have about doing so?

FOURTH CUP OF WINE

Lift the fourth cup of wine and read together.

וְלָקַחְתִּי אֶתְכֶם ...   V'lakachti etchem ...   I will redeem you ...

בָּרוּךְ אַתָּה יְיָ,
אֱלֹהֵינוּ מֶלֶךְ הָעוֹלָם,
בּוֹרֵא פְּרִי הַגָּפֶן.

Baruch Atah Adonai,
Eloheinu Melech ha'olam,
borei p'ree hagafen.

Blessed are You, our God, Ruler of the Universe, who creates the fruit of the vine.

When we rise up from our Seder tables, let us commit ourselves to stamping out xenophobia and hatred in every place that it persists. Echoing God's words when God said, "I take you to be my people," let us say to those who seek safety in our midst, "we take you to be our people." May we see past difference and dividing lines and remember, instead, that we were all created *b'tzelem Elohim*, in the image of God. May we see welcoming the stranger at our doorstep not as a danger but an opportunity – to enrich the fabric of our country, to deepen our experience of the world around us, and to live out our Jewish values in action. Blessed are You, Adonai Our God, who has created us all in Your image.

Drink the fourth cup of wine.

ZEROAH

Leader: As we conclude our Seder this evening, we draw our attention to the final item on our Seder plate. The *zeroah* (shank bone), which literally means "arm," reminds us of the "outstretched arm" with which God brought the Israelite people out of slavery in Egypt.[26]

Jewish tradition teaches us that we are God's partners in the continual act of creating a more just world in which all human beings are treated with dignity and compassion. As we recall the strength that God extended to the Jewish people in the season of our escape from oppression, we extend *our* arms to embrace those in our world still experiencing persecution because of who they are.

May tonight's Seder inspire each of us to take action on behalf of today's refugees and asylum seekers, as we join and strengthen the Jewish response to the global refugee crisis at this critical moment in history.

NIRTZAH ן

Before you conclude the Seder and say the words "next year in Jerusalem," read this section and perform the closing ritual – the fifth communal cup.

Leader: At the beginning of the Passover Seder, we are commanded to consider ourselves as though we, too, had gone out from Egypt. At the end of the Seder (and once in the middle) – we say the words, "Next year in Jerusalem" to recognize that, just as redemption came for our ancestors, so, too, will redemption come for us in this generation. For those of us fortunate enough to have a roof over our heads, we may understand these words to mean that the parts of us that feel adrift will find steady footing. However, for the world's more than 68 million displaced people and refugees, these words can be a literal message of hope that they will be able to rebuild their lives in a safe place.

Participant: After experiencing unimaginable trauma and often making harrowing journeys out of danger, refugees across the United States are finding liberation after oppression. For Mohammad Ay Toghlo and his wife, Eidah Al Suleiman, the dream of "Next year in Jerusalem" has become a reality in Buffalo, New York. After war came to their village outside Damascus, they witnessed the murder of their pregnant daughter and the kidnapping of their son. They sold their car to pay a large ransom and then ultimately escaped to Lebanon. After a lengthy vetting process, Mohammed, Eidah, and their youngest son, Najati, received word they would be resettled by HIAS through the Jewish Family Service of Buffalo. Mohammed says that, when he found out, he thought he was dreaming because "the United States is such a big thing for us that I don't even see that in my dreams; I was so happy." Najati is learning English and enrolled

in school, and he says that, when he finds himself on the street on the way to school or to an appointment and he needs assistance, people go out of their way to communicate with him and help, even reading his body language to try to understand what he needs. While the family's move is bittersweet because their oldest son, daughter-in-law, and grandchildren remain in Lebanon and they worry constantly about their safety, Najati says that, here, in the United States, "wherever we go, we find helpful, loving people." As he settles into his new life here, Najati made a drawing to express his gratitude for the opportunities that the Jewish Family Service of Buffalo and the United States government have provided him and his family. The drawing expresses thanks to the United States and features a large Jewish star, surrounded by the phrase "Thank you, Jewish Family" in Arabic. The family's life in Buffalo is not free from difficulty, but they are beginning to pick up the broken pieces of the trauma they have experienced to fulfill new hopes and new dreams here in America.

Group: As we now end the Seder, let us pass around a fifth cup into which we will each pour a drop of wine as we express our prayers for the world's refugees.

Pass an empty wine glass around the Seder table and have everyone add a drop of wine from their untasted cup (from the "Kavanah for Opening the Door for Elijah") into this new communal cup. After everyone has added some wine to this fifth communal cup, read this blessing aloud together:

Tonight, we honor the strength and resilience of refugees and asylum seekers across the globe. We commit ourselves to supporting them as they rebuild their lives and to championing their right for protection. Just as our own people now eat the bread of liberation, we pray that today's refugees and asylum seekers will fulfill their dreams of rebuilding their lives in safety and freedom in the year to come.

Blessed are all those who yearn to be free.

Blessed are we who commit ourselves to their freedom.

Blessed are You, Adonai Our God, source of strength and liberation.

לְשָׁנָה הַבָּאָה בִּירוּשָׁלָיִם!

L'shana ha'ba'ah b'Yirushalayim!

HOW YOU CAN HELP

The American Jewish movement for refugees is vibrant and strong. You can get involved by educating yourself and others, speaking up, taking to the streets, volunteering, organizing your community to take action, and/or donating to support HIAS' work helping refugees rebuild their lives in the U.S. and around the world.

*Visit **hias.org/take-action** for more information about all of these ways to help refugees.*

REFERENCES

1. https://www.cnn.com/2017/01/03/asia/myanmar-alan-kurdi/index.html (Accessed February 2019).
2. http://www.dailymail.co.uk/news/article-3279160/Heartbreaking-moment-mother-clutching-lifeless-body-six-month-old-baby-plucked-Mediterranean-10-migrants-spotted-yacht-crew.html (Accessed February 2019).
3. https://www.cbsnews.com/news/migrants-deliberately-drowned-yemen-shabwa-beach-international-organization-migration/ (Accessed February 2019).
4. https://joelartista.com/syrian-refugees-the-zaatari-project-jordan/ (Accessed February 2019).
5. Sarah Dryden-Peterson, *The Educational Experiences of Refugee Children in Countries of First Asylum* (Washington DC: Migration Policy Institute, 2015), 1.
6. http://www.huffingtonpost.com/2015/06/23/syrian-refugee-women-documentary_n_7638290.html (Accessed February 2019).
7. https://techfugees.com/news/translation-through-text-how-nowall-can-help-refugees-overcome-the-language-barrier/ (Accessed February 2019).
8. The 1951 Refugee Convention is a multilateral treaty that defines who is a refugee, outlines the rights of refugees, and describes the obligations of the countries that grant asylum.
9. https://asylumaccess.org/wp-content/uploads/2014/09/FINAL_Global-Refugee-Work-Rights-Report-2014_Interactive.pdf (Accessed February 2019).
10. *ibid.*
11. Pseudonym used to protect the client's safety.
12. https://www.hias.org/blog/watch-food-and-friendship-recipe-humanity (Accessed February 2019).
13. Hamid's story via UNHCR.
14. http://www.hias.org/sites/default/files/hias_-_triple_jeopardy_-_full_report.pdf (Accessed February 2019).
15. https://www.washingtonpost.com/news/in-sight/wp/2015/10/14/they-made-the-long-rough-journey-to-cross-the-u-s-border-alone-here-are-their-faces-and-voices/ (Accessed February 2019).
16. https://dash.harvard.edu/bitstream/handle/1/23989485/dryden-peterson2015RefugeeEdBreakingOpen.pdf?sequence=1 (Accessed February 2019).
17. Muna's story via UNHCR.
18. The stories of Um, Sajida, and Muhammed come from http://www.mercycorps.org/photoessays/jordan-syria/we-asked-refugees-what-did-you-bring-you. Their photos are reprinted with the permission of photographer Sumaya Agha (http://www.sumayaagha.net/).
19. The stories of Magboola and Dowla come from http://petapixel.com/2013/03/21/portraits-of-refugees-posing-with-their-most-valued-possessions (accessed February 2019). Their photos are reprinted with the permission of UNHCR and photographer Brian Sokol (http://www.briansokol.com).
20. Farhad's story comes from https://petapixel.com/2016/08/26/portraits-refugees-precious-possession/ (accessed February 2019).
21. http://www.newamericaneconomy.org/wp-content/uploads/2017/06/NAE_Refugees_V5.pdf (Accessed February 2019).
22. *ibid.*
23. https://www.npr.org/sections/goatsandsoda/2017/12/25/572835450/how-a-liberian-refugee-got-to-be-a-montana-mayor (Accessed February 2019).
24. https://www.acf.hhs.gov/orr/success-story/programs/orr/refugee-voices/programs/orr/refugee-voices/sam-yamin (Accessed February 2019).
25. Excerpts from Nathaly Rosas Martinez, "Where Food is an Art," in Merna Ann Hecht, ed., *Our Table of Memories: Food & Poetry of Spirit, Homeland, & Tradition* (Seattle, WA: Chatwin Books, 2015), 49-50.
26. Deuteronomy 26:8.

Compiled by and with original liturgical content written by Rabbi Rachel Grant Meyer
Illustration and design by Hillel Smith

Made in the USA
Middletown, DE
17 April 2019